PRO WRESTLING LEGENDS

CHELSEA HOUSE PUBLISHERS

Shawn Michaels: The Story of the Wrestler They Call "The Heartbreak Kid"

Stephen Ciacciarelli

Chelsea House Publishers
Philadelphia

Produced by Chestnut Productions and Choptank Syndicate, Inc.

Editor and Picture Researcher: Mary Hull
Design and Production: Lisa Hochstein

CHELSEA HOUSE PUBLISHERS

Editor in Chief: Sally Cheney
Associate Editor in Chief: Kim Shinners
Production Manager: Pamela Loos
Art Director: Sara Davis
Director of Photography: Judy L. Hasday

Cover Photos: The Acci'Dent

The Chelsea House World Wide Web site
address is http://www.chelseahouse.com

First Printing

1 3 5 7 9 8 6 4 2

Library of Congress Cataloging-in-Publication Data

Ciacciarelli, Stephen.
    Shawn Michaels : the story of the wrestler they call "the Heartbreak Kid: / Stephen
    Ciacciarelli.
        p. cm. — (Pro wrestling legends)
    Includes bibliographical references.
    ISBN 0–7910–6453–0 (alk. paper) — ISBN 0–7910–6454–9 (pbk. : alk. paper)
        1. Michaels, Shawn. 2. Wrestlers—United States—Biography. I. Title. II. Series.

GV1196.M53 C53 2001
796.812'092—dc21
[B]
                                                                        2001028084

Contents

1 TRIPLE CROWN WINNER

here was electricity in the air as the World Wrestling Federation (WWF) premier event of the year, Wrestle-Mania XII, got underway on March 31, 1996, at The Pond in Anaheim, California. The 18,852 fans in attendance were primed for the most exciting wrestling card of the year.

The WWF's annual extravaganza always generated plenty of excitement, but this year there was even a stronger buzz in the air as the main event pitted two of the federation's greatest technical wrestlers against each other in one of the sport's most grueling contests. Challenger Shawn Michaels, by virtue of winning the 1996 Royal Rumble, was getting his chance to win the WWF World heavyweight championship from three-time champ Bret "the Hitman" Hart, one of the most decorated wrestlers in the sport.

Michaels's record was not too shabby either, as he came into the event as a three-time WWF Intercontinental champion and two-time tag team champ. Still, Hart had more experience and was the defending champion, so Shawn, despite all his talent and determination, was the underdog.

The 6' 1", 235-pounder with the blue-green eyes and long blond hair was the fan favorite, however, having earned a reputation as one of the sport's high-flyers. Michaels boasted an

---

Michaels holds up his first WWF World heavyweight championship belt in triumph after his victory over Bret Hart in an Iron Man match held on March 31, 1996, at WrestleMania XII.

arsenal of aerial ring maneuvers of the type used in the Mexican style of wrestling. He had also earned the reputation of a maverick who laughs in the face of adversity, so he took it all in stride when then-WWF commissioner "Rowdy" Roddy Piper declared that Shawn's match against Bret was to be a 60-minute "Iron Man match!"

An Iron Man match! The thought of it was enough to keep most wrestlers in the locker room. The stipulations were that the match was to continue for the full 60-minute time limit. At the end of 60 minutes, the man with the most decisions would be declared the winner. Decisions could occur by pinfall, submission, countout, or disqualification. Simply put, it was truly a grueling event.

Shawn was ready, however. The charismatic and flamboyant wrestler who had become known as "the Heartbreak Kid," had been waiting for this moment for 18 years. When Shawn was just a boy of 12 years old he had dreamed of becoming the WWF World champion, and it was now time for him to live his dream.

"For the first time ever, I can't really think of a whole lot to say," Shawn said in an interview on the WrestleMania XII telecast before the match. "Everybody knows the story. Now is the time for the final chapter."

His opponent was one of the most skilled wrestlers in the sport, known as "the Excellence of Execution." Bret, a second-generation wrestler taught by his father, himself a former champion, claimed to be "The best there is, the best there was, and the best there will ever be."

The match had all the makings of a classic. Shawn's entrance music blared throughout the arena. The crowd rose to its feet and cheered as they waited to get a glimpse of Shawn coming to the ring. Shawn's mentor, Jose Lothario, made his way to the squared circle, and although the crowd waited patiently, there was no sign of Michaels. Suddenly, Jose pointed to the rafters and the audience looked up to where a spotlight shone on a solitary figure. There, 100 feet in the air, was the man they call the Heartbreak Kid!

Shawn waved to the cheering crowd, which began to ooh and aah as he proceeded to drop from the ceiling! Shawn was attached to a cable, and he glided down to the wrestling ring like an exotic bird, making one of the most dramatic entrances in ring history. The fans were still buzzing as he detached himself from the cable and entered the ring.

Bret's more traditional entrance paled in comparison, but he was wearing the coveted championship belt and seemed to be all business as he entered the squared circle. He kissed the gold belt before handing it over to the referee. Color commentator Jerry "the King" Lawler joked that Bret "might be kissing that belt goodbye." Shawn could only hope so!

The referee explained the rules to the two combatants as the crowd hushed in anticipation of the opening bell. When it rang out, Shawn and Bret immediately locked up and the much-awaited battle was underway.

Before the match, Bret had admitted that he had planned to beat Shawn into submission, keep him on the mat, and take away his high-flying aerial maneuvers. In the early going, however, it was Shawn who was the aggressor and, being slightly quicker than Bret, he was

Bret Hart grimaces in pain as Michaels twists his arm. Both men struggled to keep their energy up during their grueling match, which was over an hour long.

able to match him move for move. Everyone seemed surprised when Shawn took a page out of Bret's book and exhibited a strong command of the basics. In the early going, it was actually Bret who took to the air more often than the usually high-flying Shawn.

As the match neared the 15-minute mark, neither of these great athletes seemed to dominate, and the advantage switched back and forth between them. Then Bret managed to slam Shawn to the mat. When he struggled to his feet, Bret clotheslined the still dazed Michaels, sending him flying backward over the top rope and out of the ring. The ref began to count Shawn out, and it looked like the first decision was imminent—but then Bret jumped out of the ring and continued the attack.

Shawn slammed Bret into the ringpost, and the dizzy Hart fell back into the timekeeper's lap. Shawn came running and delivered a superkick, but Bret leapt out of the way and the timekeeper took the blow full-force, falling to the floor unconscious. A true melee was underway.

The battle returned to the ring, where Shawn concentrated his attention on weakening Bret's left shoulder. When Bret had the advantage, he worked on Shawn's neck and lower back. The competent grapplers traded moves and countermoves, causing Lawler to comment, "I'm surprised! I thought Shawn would be jumping around like a Mexican jumping bean! He's doing the complete opposite of what Bret thought he would do."

At the 30-minute mark, both wrestlers were exhausted. There were a couple of near pinfalls, but neither man could gain a decision. It looked as if Bret might be the first to gain a decision after he was able to give Shawn a piledriver, but Shawn recovered enough to shove Bret into the corner of the ring. He got a running start and leapt on Bret, who managed to flip Shawn over the top rope and out of the ring.

Shawn wound up getting thrown out of the ring a few more times, and twice he knocked down his mentor, Lothario, who appeared dazed and had to rest his head on the ring apron. The wrestlers, however, had to continue as the 45-minute mark passed.

At one point, Bret was able to set up a stunned Shawn on the top turnbuckle and administer a standing reverse suplex. OUCH!

With Shawn writhing in pain on the mat, Bret went in for the kill, attempting to trap Shawn in his signature finisher, a submission move known as the "sharpshooter." A well-placed kick by Shawn thwarted the maneuver. Bret was able to counter with a Boston crab, however, and it looked like Shawn might be forced to submit. Shawn, in great pain, was able to inch his way closer to the ring ropes and grab the lowest one, forcing Bret to break the hold.

The one-hour time limit was quickly approaching, and neither man had yet to gain a decision! In desperation Bret attempted a flying leap off the top rope onto the prone Shawn. It looked grim for Michaels, but he lifted his legs and was able to deliver a knee to Bret's face. With Hart dazed, Shawn rebounded, getting "his 19th wind," according to Lawler, and nearly scoring a pin with 2 minutes and 50 seconds remaining. This match was going down to the wire!

Although each man was clearly hurt, they battled to a series of near falls at 2:15, 1:50 and 1:20, and the clocked ticked on. With only 40 seconds left to go, Shawn leapt off the top rope, but Bret was able to catch him, slam him to the mat, and clamp on the sharpshooter.

It looked like the end. Although he cried out in pain, Michaels refused to throw in the towel. He held on until the final bell rang, and Bret was forced to release the hold. The time limit had been reached and there was no winner . . . or was there?

Bret made it clear that he thought he was still the champion. After all, he hadn't been beaten, so he reasoned that he should retain the championship belt. The referee seemed to agree, and he handed Bret the title belt while Shawn was still writhing in pain on the canvas.

Bret was actually out of the ring and on his way back to the locker room when a commotion took place in the ring. WWF President Gorilla Monsoon conferred with the referee and then made a decision: The match must continue under sudden death rules! That meant the man who gained the first decision in overtime was the winner.

This didn't sit well with Bret, who was obviously upset. When the match restarted, the Hitman went on the attack, taking it to the still-suffering Michaels, hammering him from pillar

When Gorilla Monsoon ruled that Shawn's match with WWF World champion Bret Hart could continue under sudden death rules, Shawn was able to martial his strength and finally knock Hart out.

to post. After he was thrown into the corner by Bret, Shawn was able to gain a reversal and managed to partially connect with a superkick to Bret's jaw. Bret hit the mat, but Shawn was too woozy to cover him for the pin. When each man struggled to his feet, Bret was surprised to be on the receiving end of one of Shawn's signature moves, known as "sweet chin music." Shawn connected solidly and Bret hit the canvas like a ton of bricks. Shawn wasted no time in covering him while the ref made the count, "one-two-three," and the crowd erupted.

The noise was deafening as the crowd roared and the Heartbreak Kid's music began to play. Bret lay dazed on the mat as the screaming fans acknowledged the new WWF World heavyweight champion, Shawn Michaels.

Shawn almost couldn't believe it himself. This moment was 18 years in the making.

As a disgusted Hart left the ring, Shawn was handed the title belt. On the verge of tears, he looked at it lovingly and kissed it. He held it up for all the fans to see, and at that moment, fireworks began to explode from the upper region of The Pond. Shawn strapped the belt around his waist and turned to each side of the ring, thanking the fans who had supported him. Then, feeling sufficiently recovered, he began to celebrate in the ring, showing off in a manner befitting not only a world champion, but also a Triple Crown winner, for Shawn had joined the elite club of those who had won three of the WWF's four championships in the course of their careers. It truly was a remarkable feat, and Michaels had achieved it the hard way.

While the celebration continued, mat experts realized that Shawn was setting out on a journey he might not be ready for—that of the WWF World champion. But the skeptics did not know Shawn Michaels. One thing the Heartbreak Kid would prove over the course of his illustrious career was that he certainly did have the heart of a champion!

2 THE EARLY YEARS

Shawn Michaels was born Michael Shawn Hickenbottom at Williams Air Force Base in Scottsdale, Arizona, on July 22, 1965. His family moved to San Antonio, Texas, when he was very young. Growing up in the south Texas town, Shawn became a wrestling fan at an early age.

While he wasn't the biggest kid on the block, he also wasn't the smallest, and young Shawn demonstrated plenty of athletic ability. He played on the football team, but there was another sport that captured his fancy and let him stand out as an individual.

"I saw wrestling for the first time when I was 12 years old—the first time I was able to stay up late—and it hit me just like that," Shawn told reporters. "From that point on, wrestling never drifted from my thoughts. I continued to play football until I graduated, but it was always in the back of my mind that I was going to be WWF champion—champion of the entire world."

But before he could take on the top talent in the WWF, Shawn had to learn his craft. San Antonio is a city near the Mexican border and has a large Tejano (Mexican-American) population. So it comes as no surprise that the area's biggest wrestling personality was Tejano wrestler Jose Lothario. To

From the time he was 12 years old Shawn knew he wanted to be a professional wrestler. Beginning at age 18, Shawn trained with wrestler Jose Lothario in San Antonio, California.

become the best, young Shawn realized, you have to learn from the best. When he turned 18 years old Shawn sought out Lothario, and, with his parents' blessings, he began training for a career in professional wrestling.

He trained hard and showed a natural ability for the mat sport. Shawn seemed to pick up the moves and countermoves easily, and it wasn't long before he was ready for his first professional match. He made his pro debut in 1984, squaring off against Art Cruz on a Mid-South Wrestling card promoted by Bill Watts. Although Shawn lost the match, he showed the determination and fire that would serve him well in his chosen profession. In his second match, the man who was now known as Shawn Michaels wrestled to a time-limit draw, showing improvement in his technique and in his won-lost record. With his third match, Michaels notched his first win. With his confidence overflowing, there was no looking back!

Michaels wrestled in the Mid-South promotion for six months, learning new moves and growing both physically and mentally. Ready for some new challenges, he took to the road and ended up in Kansas City, Missouri, where Bob Geigel, the former National Wrestling Alliance (NWA) Central States champion, ran the territory. Geigel was also a former tag team champion, and he introduced Shawn to the team aspect of the sport. Under Geigel's guidance, Michaels learned the intricacies of tag team wrestling, including how to work together with a partner to get the best results.

Michaels's stint in Kansas City was important for another reason. It was there that he met another up-and-coming wrestler by the

Marty Jannetty first met up with Shawn Michaels in Kansas City, Missouri, where they both wrestled for a small promotion run by former NWA champion Bob Geigel.

name of Marty Jannetty. But before they could join forces, Shawn was on the move again, coming back to his home state to wrestle for Texas All-Star Wrestling.

With his new-found tag team skills and Geigel's instructions still buzzing around in his head, Michaels decided to concentrate on the tag team division of the promotion. He took on

Paul Diamond as his partner and together they wrestled as "the American Force." They quickly established an image for themselves as true American patriots. The two young wrestlers worked well together, and soon they were in the running for the promotion's tag team title.

Shawn and Paul's first title reign came as a gift from Eddie Guerrero, literally! Guerrero had won the Texas All-Star tag team title belt from his former partner Al Madril in a singles match and, rather than picking a partner, he gave the belts to Michaels and Diamond on September 1, 1985. Less than a month later, on September 29th, the Masked Hoods (Ricky Santana and Tony Torres) beat the American Force

Early in his career, Michaels earned a reputation as a high-flying aerial wrestler who was comfortable leaping off the ropes. He developed a signature flying kick that came to be known as "sweet chin music."

for the championship. Michaels and Diamond were determined to win the belts back and they did in a rematch on November 17th. The dynamic duo of Shawn and Paul successfully defended the title until January 27, 1986, when their second title reign was ended by Al Madril and Magnificent Zulu. Although they had lost the belts they had fought so hard for, Shawn and Paul had served notice that they were a force to be reckoned with and should never be underestimated.

That wasn't enough for Michaels, though. He had other things on his mind. While Diamond was an excellent partner, and there was nothing wrong with being super patriotic, Michaels wanted to establish a more contemporary image, something which would appeal to the youth of America. Fortunately for Michaels, there was another young man in the promotion with the same thing on his mind. His name was Marty Jannetty, and he joined forces with Michaels to change the face of tag team wrestling.

3 | THE ROCKERS!

One of Michaels's early mentors was Ricky Morton, the dynamic blond half of the Rock 'n' Roll Express, a very successful tag team in the early 1980s. By the mid-1980s the most cohesive team in the country was the Midnight Express. This team consisted of "Beautiful" Bobby Eaton and "Loverboy" Dennis Condrey (later replaced by "Sweet" Stan Lane). Michaels and Jannetty wanted to emulate the precision two-man attacks, speed moves, and slick tags of both Expresses. They named their team the Midnight Rockers.

The Midnight Rockers were an instant success and quickly won the NWA Central States Tag Team Championship, beating the Batten twins, Brad and Bart, for the title on May 15, 1986. Despite working together like a well-oiled machine, Michaels and Jannetty were only able to hold on to the coveted title belts for a week before losing them to the Battens again on May 22nd.

The Midnight Rockers battled on, perfecting their teamwork and developing new strategies to throw their opponents off track. They were unable to regain the Central States Tag Team titles, but they felt confident enough to move on and step into the spotlight with the American Wrestling Association

Calling themselves the Midnight Rockers, Marty Jannetty, left, and Shawn Michaels, right, wrestled first in the NWA and then the AWA, where they earned two tag team championships before moving up to the WWF in 1988.

(AWA) where they gained some much-needed national exposure.

By 1986 much of the spark of the once-mighty AWA was gone. After all this was the promotion that once boasted such world champions as Verne Gagne, Nick Bockwinkel, and "Mad Dog" Vachon, as well as tag team greats like Crusher and Dick the Bruiser, Larry Hennig and Harley Race, and Hard Boiled Haggerty and Gene Kiniski. But while the league faded, the Midnight Rockers shined, eventually winning the AWA tag titles on January 27, 1987, and fiercely warring with the treacherous twosome of "Playboy" Buddy Rose and Doug Somers.

"Marty and I think alike," Michaels told *Wrestling World* magazine at the time. "We

Ricky Morton, left, the blond half of the Rock 'n' Roll Express, was one of Shawn Michaels's role models.

always know what each other is thinking," he continued, explaining their success. As the champions, the Midnight Rockers got plenty of television time and people around the country began to sit up and take notice. Young, good looking, and energetic, not to mention success-ful, the Midnight Rockers captured the fancy of young wrestling fans across the land. Inspired by cheerleading announcer Larry Nelson, the audience enthusiastically responded to the dynamic duo.

All good things must come to an end, and the Midnight Rockers's AWA title reign ended on May 25, 1987, when they were beaten by Russian terrors Soldat Ustinov and Boris Zhukov. The boys didn't spend too much time worrying about their loss. Instead, they accepted an offer from the World Wrestling Federation (WWF) and flew to a TV taping. Unfortunately, the excited duo was a little too rambunctious for their new employer, and Michaels and Jannetty were fired the next day.

Although their WWF sojourn was a short one, it was another notch in their belts. When they returned to the AWA they began a long-term feud with the RPMs (Mike Davis and Tommy Lane) and won the Southern tag team championship from them on October 26. The RPMs rallied, however, and regained the presti-gious championship on November 16. Not to be outdone, Michaels and Jannetty bounced back even more quickly, capturing their second Southern tag team championship just days later on November 22.

Things were looking good for the Midnight Rockers, and they were basking in their popu-larity. The duo began to get a reputation for being cocky—especially Shawn—whose good looks and sparkling blue-green eyes made him extremely popular with female fans. At 6' 1" and 233 pounds, Shawn was average-sized and thus able to avoid the "freak show" label that burdened some of the sport's larger competitors. He stayed in excellent physical shape and was one of the more agile wrestlers in the ring. The brief taste of the big time stuck with Shawn long after he left the WWF. So he kept a high profile in the AWA while he figured out a way to get back into the WWF and live out his dream of becoming WWF World champion.

In the meantime he and Jannetty continued to make strides as a team, constantly learning and adding new dimensions to their ring tactics. Their hard work paid off when the boys won their second AWA World tag team championship on December 27, 1987, as they beat the original Midnight Express. Unfortunately, this victory meant they had to relinquish the Southern tag team championship, as the Southern promotion wouldn't allow them to hold two sets of title belts. Naturally, they kept the more prestigious of the two titles.

The Midnight Rockers were sitting on top of the AWA world. Shawn was the promotion's most popular competitor, and he couldn't wait to move on. So, it was a blessing in disguise when Badd Company, the team of Paul Diamond and Pat Tanaka, ended the Midnight Rockers' second AWA World tag team title reign on March 19, 1988.

It was indeed a blessing. The WWF was interested in this high-flying duo again, and the time was ripe for Michaels and Jannetty to leave the AWA behind and head back to the

WWF, the acknowledged number-one promotion in the nation. WWF scouts, impressed with the boys' televised AWA matches, had invited the Rockers to compete against federation superstars. They encouraged Shawn to grow his hair long and adopt an MTV-type image. Michaels and Jannetty dropped the "Midnight" from their moniker to avoid confusion (and potential legal ramifications) with the Midnight Express, who were then working for rival NWA boss Jim Crockett. And so, the Rockers were born in 1988.

"I've always set my goals very high. I want to be very big," Shawn told *Wrestling World* magazine. "But [for me] wrestling in the WWF is a dream come true."

Shawn and Marty were now facing much larger and tougher opponents than they had in the past. Still, they continued their winning ways. Always in the hunt for the WWF championship, they faced formidable tag teams like the Hart Foundation and Demolition. They feuded with the Rougeau Brothers and the team of Arn Anderson and Tully Blanchard. With each match, the Rockers showcased their skills as one of the most technically proficient tag teams in the sport.

In 1990 the Rockers feuded with Power & Glory (Hercules and Paul Roma), and Michaels was injured when Hercules used a chain on his knee. He recovered sufficiently to participate in a match against the Hart Foundation for the WWF World tag team title. The Rockers won the match but not the title—the top rope broke during the bout and the WWF did not acknowledge a title change. Still, the match ranked the Rockers as one of the federation's premier tag teams. As the Rockers became a more promi-nent team, Michaels's confidence slowly turned to arrogance.

"Let's just face the facts, it took me a while, but I finally realized just how great I am," Shawn bragged to *Wrestling World.* "I am the best looking wrestler in the business. I am young, in great physical condition, strong, extremely fast, agile, [and] experienced. I have absolutely everything going for me. I am everything that a champion pro wrestler could want."

Still, the tag-team wars called and Michaels had to put aside his desire for individual glory and concentrate on teamwork. A feud with Orient Express culminated at the WWF's Royal Rumble extravaganza in 1991 with a victory for the Rockers. After a loss at the Survivor Series, however, Shawn began grumbling, and he blamed the loss on Marty.

"Let's forget about that night," Jannetty said to Michaels in a Wrestling World article. "Let's forget these differences of opinions. We have one of the greatest tag teams in wrestling."

Jannetty was shorter and stockier than Michaels and was considered the tougher of the two, but Shawn performed more of the flashy techniques that tended to capture the crowd's attention. The more victories the Rockers totaled up, the more Michaels took credit for them.

Although the general public was unaware of it, insiders knew all was not well in the Rockers's camp. Rumors circulated. Supposedly, the men refused to have anything to do with each other outside the ring, and even went so far as to arrive at arenas in separate cars.

Finally, Shawn and Marty's personal animos-ity came to a head. During a "Brutus Beefcake's

Barber Shop" television interview in 1992, Michaels stunned the team's supporters when he superkicked Jannetty right through the set's window glass! That definitely signaled the end of the Rockers as a team.

4 THE HEARTBREAK KID

Having turned on his partner in a dramatic fashion, Michaels compared the breakup of the Rockers to Phil Collins leaving the rock group Genesis and beginning to forge his way ahead on the solo circuit. In early 1992 he hired on "Sensational" Sherri Martel as his manager and took on the nickname "the Heartbreak Kid." Michaels was just 27 years old and ready to rocket into the big time.

"We weren't the tag team specialists, I was the tag team specialist—it was ALL ME," Shawn told *Wrestling World* in February 1995. "But that is old news; the fact is, I am one of the fastest, most capable wrestlers in the sport. I have an excellent amateur wrestling background as well, as you can tell by my style."

In addition to his wrestling prowess, which included dazzling aerial maneuvers, Michaels proved to be a natural on the microphone—an all-important factor on the modern wrestling scene. Shawn began to play up his bad guy image and rile the fans. He was not just cocky, he was downright arrogant. Not only that, he considered himself the most hand-some man in the sport, and he let the crowd know it! Sherri insisted mirrors be placed all around the ring so Shawn could

---

One of the most dramatic ladder matches ever took place on March 20, 1994, when Michaels faced Razor Ramon at WrestleMania X in New York.

admire himself whenever he wanted. Of course this only made the fans howl at the Heartbreak Kid even more.

In mid-1992 when he got his own WWF talk show segment, "The Heartbreak Hotel," on WWF broadcasts, Shawn became the most celebrated heel in the WWF for his remarks about himself as well as other wrestlers. Luckily for Michaels, not only could he talk the talk, he could walk the walk, backing up his words with action in the ring. He was, plainly put, the man the fans loved to hate.

When the Heartbreak Kid began his singles career in the WWF he hired "Sensational" Sherri Martel as his manager, but even she couldn't put up with his selfish ways for very long.

"I don't mind when people say I'm snotty, stuck up, conceited, whatever you want to call it," Shawn admitted to *Wrestling World.* " In fact, deep inside, I kind of like it."

Sherri stood by Michaels, often interfering in matches to ensure that he emerged victorious. The brash Heartbreak Kid quickly inserted himself into the WWF title picture, feuding with Bret "the Hitman" Hart over the federation's intercontinental title. The two men, considered the best technical wrestlers in the federation, battled back and forth throughout the spring and summer in some thrilling matches, but Michaels was unable to take the belt from the more experienced Hart.

Michaels was making other enemies as well. He became embroiled in another feud with Rick "the Model" Martel over who had the right to have Sherri in his corner. The feud culminated at SummerSlam in London, England, on August 30, 1992, when Shawn and Rick fought to a double count-out.

The Heartbreak Kid re-entered the title picture when Bret Hart lost the intercontinental title to the British Bulldog, aka Davey Boy Smith. Having failed to take the belt from Bret previously, Michaels felt he had a better chance against the Bulldog. He got that chance on October 27, 1992, on the nationally televised "Saturday Night's Main Event." In what many experts deemed the Match of the Year, Michaels battled the ferocious Bulldog and came away with the WWF Intercontinental title. It was his first taste of gold in the WWF.

Even with the gold belt strapped around his waist, Michaels still wasn't happy. In fact, he seemed to be more brash and cocky than ever.

"Women fall in love with me quickly, men envy me and are jealous of me, and promoters are always after me because I draw a big crowd," said Michaels. He immediately challenged the WWF World champion, who happened to be none other than Bret Hart.

Just a month after winning the intercontinental title, Michaels squared off against Bret in a world title match at the WWF's 1992 Survivor Series. Unfortunately for Shawn, he did not win the belt. The match did, however, go down in the record books as one of the classics, and it stoked the fire of revenge in Shawn. From this point on, there seemed to be nothing but bad blood between Michaels and Hart.

Michaels still had the WWF Intercontinental title, however, and that was enough to lure his old partner Marty Jannetty back to competition in the WWF. Marty was out for revenge and he attempted to smash a mirror over Michaels's head. Shawn wisely got out of the way, using Sherri to block the blow. Sherri took a direct hit as Michaels scurried out of the ring. This incident officially ended Sherri's partnership with Shawn! So it was no surprise that when Michaels faced Jannetty at the Royal Rumble in Sacramento, California, on January 24, 1993, Sherri was in Marty's corner! It didn't matter, however, as Michaels still prevailed.

In addition to Jannetty, Michaels also had to fend off the challenges of Tatanka, the Native American warrior. Tatanka seemed to have the inside track on the intercontinental title, as he was able to beat Shawn in tag team and nontitle matches. Unfortunately for the gallant Tatanka, he was never able to get the job done when it counted.

These successful title defenses made Michaels even cockier, if that was possible. While being interviewed on the May 17, 1993, broadcast of *Monday Night Raw*, Shawn claimed that he could beat anyone, anyplace, at anytime. As soon as he had finished uttering those words, Jannetty arrived on the scene and challenged Michaels. Of course, Michaels had to accept. The match took place later in the evening and Jannetty emerged victorious, stripping the big-mouthed Michaels of his coveted intercontinental title.

Shawn was anything but humbled, however. With more enemies than ever, he decided it would be wise to hire a bodyguard. His choice was a 7', 300-pound giant named Diesel, who had ring experience from his stint as "Vinnie

Wrestling commentators called it the Match of the Year on October 27, 1992, when Michaels challenged British Bulldog "Davey Boy" Smith for the WWF Intercontinental title and won.

Vegas" in World Championship Wrestling (WCW).

At this time, Michaels rivaled Bret Hart as the WWF's most versatile athlete. And he would be the first to tell you that! Bolstered by his bodyguard, the self-proclaimed Heartbreak Kid became unbearable. Diesel became Shawn's ace in the hole. When his rematch against Marty Jannetty came up on June 6, 1993, Michaels brought Diesel along and the mammoth hired hand made sure Shawn won the match—and the WWF Intercontinental belt—from Jannetty.

As Michaels embarked on his second intercontinental title reign, the roles were clear-cut: Shawn was the star, Diesel—nicknamed "Big Daddy Cool"—was the muscle. Swallowing his pride, Diesel accepted those stipulations. For the time being . . .

Diesel helped Michaels repel the challenge of Curt "Mr. Perfect" Hennig, but in September 1993 Michaels was stripped of his title when he didn't defend it within a 30-day period. Insiders claim it was more of a contractual problem between Michaels and the WWF. The fans will probably never know the true story, but he remained out of action for a while and kept an uncharacteristically low profile.

Michaels returned to action at the WWF Survivor Series in 1993 and immediately made a new enemy in Razor Ramon. Ramon was the current intercontinental champ but Michaels laid claim to the title, maintaining that he had never been beaten for it. Michaels and Diesel began interfering in Ramon's matches, and they infuriated "the Bad Guy." Michaels cost Razor the title during his Royal Rumble match with IRS when he knocked Ramon out, although the decision was later reversed. In the Battle Royal of that same Royal Rumble, Shawn "accidentally" eliminated Diesel and the tension between the bodyguard and the wrestler began to build.

The Michaels-Ramon feud was an exciting time in WWF history, and it had some classic matches. Michaels lost a brutal ladder match to Ramon at WrestleMania X in New York City on March 20, 1994, but the bout was hailed as Match of the Year by *Pro Wrestling Illustrated*, and mat experts ranked it as one of the best WrestleMania battles ever.

Even though Michaels lost the match to Ramon, he put up an outstanding fight. Afterward, however, Shawn seemed content to sit back and let Diesel figure out how they were going to get the title back. As puzzling as it was, this plan worked. They got the belt back when Diesel won it from Ramon on April 13, 1994. The Diesel/Ramon feud continued, and Ramon regained the title from Big Daddy Cool just over four months later.

In the meantime Michaels and Diesel had begun competing as a tag team. On August 28, 1994, they defeated the Headshrinkers to become the new WWF World tag team champions! The next day, August 29, the WWF held its annual SummerSlam extravaganza. Once again Diesel faced Ramon at the event. Michaels was in Diesel's corner, as usual. Michaels also interfered, as usual, but this time their plan backfired. As Michaels attempted to give Ramon a taste of "sweet chin music," Razor moved out of the way and Diesel took the flying dropkick instead! Diesel fell to the mat, and

Despite bringing the ladder down on Razor, Michaels was unable to defeat him at WrestleMania X in 1994. But his fans didn't mind; they loved every minute of the heart-stopping action in the Michaels/Ramon feud.

Ramon covered him for the pin. Razor Ramon was the new WWF Intercontinental champ! The two men still held the tag team belts together, but the whole arena and the millions of fans watching at home could see the tension building between Diesel and Michaels.

"This could happen to anyone in the heat of battle," Michaels told Wrestling Tourbook. He shrugged off the incidents, noting that, in wrestling, emotions run high, mistakes are made, and even the best laid plans are subject to change.

But the dam of pent-up anger between Michaels and Diesel finally erupted on Thanksgiving eve, 1994. Michaels and Diesel were members of the same Survivors Series squad along with Owen Hart, Jeff Jarrett, and Jim Neidhart. Their adversaries were Razor Ramon, the 1-2-3 Kid, the Headshrinkers, and the British Bulldog. Again, Shawn set out to deliver some sweet chin music and missed, with Diesel taking the blow. Their teammates had to separate them as tempers flared.

As 1995 approached, the two tag team champions wisely decided to concentrate on the singles wrestling scene. Michaels started off 1995 on a good note. At the Royal Rumble, held January 22 in Tampa, Florida, he was the first number selected. This meant he would be the first man to enter the ring and would run the greatest risk of tiring over the course of the battle as more wrestlers continued to enter the ring. Rather than being upset at this unlucky draw, the cocky Heartbreak Kid swaggered into the ring like he was out for a walk on the beach.

The winner of the Royal Rumble was assured a shot at the WWF World heavyweight title at WrestleMania, and he would be escorted to that event by *Baywatch* star Pamela Anderson. It seemed that he was actually happy that he would have more time to spend in front of Pamela Anderson, who was on hand to see who she would be escorting to the ring at WrestleMania XI.

Thanks to some fancy footwork, he went the distance and eventually dumped runner-up Davey Boy Smith over the top rope to emerge as the winner. It was a remarkable feat. Shawn was the first man in Rumble history to be the first man in and the last man remaining.

While Michaels was having a good run, Diesel had been having an even better one. The man known also known as Big Daddy Cool had been scheduled to face former WWF champion Bob Backlund in late November and early December 1994. As luck would have it, Backlund beat Bret Hart at the Survivor Series on November 23, 1994—which meant that Big Daddy Cool fought Backlund for the world championship the weekend following the event. Diesel surprised Backlund with a jackknife immediately after the opening bell; eight seconds later, Diesel was the new WWF World champion! WWF president Jack Tunney declared the champ could not also serve as tag team champion as well, so Diesel abandoned his teammate Michaels. The tag team title was declared vacant, but that didn't bother Diesel, who was the new number-one man, in more ways than one.

Even though Diesel was the new WWF World champion, Shawn was still as cocky as ever. By virtue of winning the Royal Rumble, Michaels had earned the number-one contender berth, giving him a shot at Big Daddy Cool's belt at WrestleMania XI. For the occasion, Shawn hired yet another bodyguard. This time he enlisted a towering WWF wrestler named "Psycho" Sid, formerly known as Sid Vicious.

"I made him what he is," Michaels scoffed when asked about his upcoming match against Diesel by *Wrestling Tourbook*. "He used to watch my back when I was the WWF Intercontinental Champion. I watched his when he had it. He learned from me what it takes to be a champion. In fact, he would never even be in the business if I hadn't hired him in the first place. . . Then he had to go and ruin a good thing," Michaels continued, sounding more and more like he had a severe case of sour grapes. "We were really tight. I know all of Diesel's moves and he knows all of mine."

After the pleasure of being escorted to the ring by Pamela Anderson, disappointment and frustration set in for Michaels. Sid proved to be an ineffective bodyguard. He interfered at the wrong times and left the Heartbreak Kid to get cleanly pinned by Diesel in the middle of the ring.

The next night, on a *Monday Night Raw* broadcast, Sid's motives were made clear. He turned on Shawn and powerbombed him three times, claiming the Heartbreak Kid was stealing his spotlight. Ironically enough, it was Diesel who raced to the ring to Shawn's rescue!

After the beating Sid gave him, Michaels missed nearly a month of action. He had been the man the fans loved to hate, but those powerbombs gave Shawn the fan's sympathy, and now it was Sid who was the recipient of their hatred. Michaels became a fan favorite. He gave his supporters a treat when he beat Jeff Jarrett to win the WWF Intercontinental title for a third time on July 23, 1995. The crowd roared their approval. The Heartbreak Kid was back!

With the intercontinental belt back on his waist, Shawn began a series of title defenses against both Sid and Razor Ramon. He had another memorable ladder match with Ramon at SummerSlam '95. Shawn won this time

Though he started off as Michaels's bodyguard and tag team partner, Diesel eventually parted ways with the Heartbreak Kid to pursue his own singles career.

around though, and to prove that he was truly the Shawn of old, he defeated Sid the next night on *Monday Night Raw*! He also reteamed with Diesel as the "Dudes With Attitudes," and together they beat the tag team champs, Yokozuna and the British Bulldog, but the title never changed hands, due to a controversial decision by federation officials.

Just when Michaels's lucky star seemed to be rising, tragedy struck. In October 1995 Michaels was attacked by a group of thugs outside of a popular nightspot. He suffered serious injuries that forced him out of the action for over a month. Because Michaels was unable to defend his WWF intercontinental title, it was awarded to Dean Douglas on October 22, 1995.

When he had recovered from his injuries, Shawn suffered a second setback. A kick from Owen Hart knocked him out cold and gave him "post-concussion syndrome." He bounced back in time for the Royal Rumble, however, with his sights set on that number-one contender spot. He proved that he was 100 percent again by winning the 30-man over-the-top Battle Royal—eliminating Diesel, of all people—to emerge the victor.

This victory set the stage for Shawn's title match against Bret Hart at WrestleMania XII. That was the momentous match when "the

Heartbreak Kid" fulfilled his fantasies by not only becoming the WWF World heavyweight champion, but also one of the WWF's elite Triple Crown winners! The kid from San Antonio was certainly riding high!

THE CHAMPION

While Michaels savored his March 31, 1996, world championship victory and lived his boyhood dream of being WWF champion, his challenger Bret Hart kept a low profile. Shawn invited his friends Diesel, Razor Ramon, Hunter Hearst Helmsley (Triple H), and the former 1–2–3 Kid, now known as X-Pac, to celebrate with him. The cocky, brash group became known as the Kliq. Together they were very influential in the direction the WWF would take. These wrestlers would all be involved in the major storylines and feuds in the WWF for the immediate future.

For instance, although they were friends outside the squared circle, Diesel turned on Shawn in an attempt to wrest away the title. Unsuccessful, he gave way to the British Bulldog, who was furious at Shawn for allegedly making a pass at his wife, Diana.

"Women fall in love with me quickly," Michaels offered by way of explanation when asked about the situation by the British publication *Wrestling Tourbook.* "Everything I have done is planned out," he continued. "All of the successes have happened for a reason."

Michaels and the Bulldog engaged in a lengthy feud, but the Bulldog was unable to take the gold from around Shawn's

Shawn faced his former tag team partner "Stone Cold" Steve Austin at the 1997 King of the Ring tournament, where the two grappled their way to a double-disqualification.

waist. Vader and Mankind were also unsuccessful contenders. But the fans had had enough
of Shawn's uncaring behavior. They knew he
was only looking out for number one, so when
he faced his former bodyguard Sid at the 1996
Survivor Series, he was booed heavily. It might
have been the jeering that threw Michaels off
his game, but when Sid attacked Jose Lothario,
the Heartbreak Kid rushed to help his mentor,
giving Sid an advantage.

Sid took that advantage and hit Shawn
with a video camera, then powerbombed him,
breaking the Heartbreak Kid's spirit when
he then covered him for the pin and the world
title! Shawn was shaken, but he was also
determined to win back what he believed was
rightfully his.

He got his chance in his hometown of San
Antonio, Texas, at the 1997 Royal Rumble on
January 19. This time it was Michaels who
used a video camera to win the bout and begin
his second reign as WWF World heavyweight
champion. Winning the highest honor in
wrestling back in front of his hometown fans
made the victory that much sweeter for
Michaels, who seemed to have taken on an air
of invincibility. After all, he was beating ring
giants like Sid and Diesel, ruthless competitors
like Mankind and Razor Ramon, powerhouses
like the Bulldog, and technical-wrestling greats
like Bret Hart and Jeff Jarrett.

So it came as some surprise when Michaels
proved to be a mere mortal after all. As Wrestle-
Mania XIII approached, and many people
projected a rematch between Shawn and Bret
Hart, the wheels came off the Heartbreak Kid
Express. On February 13, 1997, on a Thursday

Raw broadcast, Shawn announced that he had "lost his smile," and thus was forfeiting the title. Wrestling fans everywhere were shocked. The seemingly invincible Shawn Michaels was forfeiting his boyhood dream because he had "lost his smile?" Impossible!

It was, however, very possible. The word among insiders was that nagging injuries, especially to one of his knees, made the Heartbreak Kid much less than 100 percent effective, and so he had decided to take some time off to recover before entering the title fray again.

The rivalry between Bret Hart, left, and Shawn was so strong it frequently spilled out of the ring and into the lockerroom.

Shawn sat on the sidelines and rehabilitated his knee. He made a surprise appearance at a March 1997 broadcast of *Monday Night Raw* and announced that he had "found his smile," claiming it was in San Antonio, where he left it. Apparently the time off did him good and recharged his batteries.

In Shawn's absence, "Stone Cold" Steve Austin had become the most popular wrestler in the WWF. So, upon Michaels's return, the Heartbreak Kid decided to play his cards right. He formed an impromptu tag team with Austin. While the two wrestlers had mixed feelings about each other, together they were the most popular tag team in the sport. The combination of Shawn's aerial tactics and Austin's brute force made them instant title contenders, and on the May 25, 1997, *Monday Night Raw* broadcast, in a match that lasted over 20 minutes, they defeated long-time champions Owen Hart and the British Bulldog to win the WWF World tag team title.

This was Michaels's second WWF World tag team title reign. His popularity soared again, at least as far as the fans were concerned. In the locker room, however, Shawn had many enemies, including the Harts. Even his partner, Austin, a notorious loner, felt threatened by the Heartbreak Kid. Austin agreed to face Michaels at the 1997 King of the Ring tournament. The teammates battled to a brutal disqualification, so nothing but bad blood emerged from that bout.

Then, on June 9, 1997, a real-life locker-room fight erupted between Bret Hart and Shawn. Michaels suffered a neck injury and aggravated his earlier knee injury. Frustrated, Michaels left the WWF, vowing never to return.

He and Stone Cold had to forfeit the tag team titles as they were unable to defend them. Fans were shocked and puzzled at Michaels's absence for the next two months.

Although Shawn had vowed never to return, he resurfaced in the WWF on August 3, acting as a special referee in the SummerSlam world title tussle between Bret Hart and the defending champion, the Undertaker. During the heated battle, the bad blood between Shawn and Bret re-emerged. Bret shoved and manhandled Michaels the referee whenever he had the chance. He even spit in Michaels's face! An infuriated Michaels grabbed a steel chair and attempted to bash Hart over the head with it. Hart nimbly moved out of the way and the Undertaker took the blow, crashing to the mat where Bret covered him. To his dismay, Shawn was forced to make the three-count. Bret Hart was declared the new WWF champion.

Michaels, however, had a few other surprises up his sleeve. Calling on his connections in the Kliq—most notably Triple H—the rulebreaking clique known as D-Generation X was born in 1997. The group, known for their total disrespect for authority, originally consisted of Michaels, Triple H, Chyna, and Rick Rude, whom Shawn had hired as "insurance." Later, "Road Dogg" Jesse James and X-Pac joined the group.

D-Generation X began feuding with the Hart Foundation, which at that time consisted of Owen Hart and the British Bulldog. Shawn set his sights on the Bulldog. The Bulldog was a native of England. So when Shawn had the opportunity to challenge Bulldog for his WWF European Championship in, of all places,

Birmingham, England, on September, 20, 1997, at the "One Night Only" pay-per-view, Shawn jumped at the chance. Sure enough, Bulldog was defeated on his native soil, and he suffered the added embarrassment of letting the Hart Foundation down. With his capture of the European title, Shawn became the first wrestler in the federation to capture all four of the WWF titles, making him a Grand Slam winner!

This did not sit well with the Bulldog's brother-in-law, Bret Hart, who found Shawn to be a real annoyance. While D-Generation X was gaining in popularity, Bret's own stature was foundering. Despite his bad guy image, Shawn

Despite being physically smaller than the Undertaker, Michaels managed to defeat him in two extraordinary matches: a "Hell in a Cell" bout in October of 1997 and an infamous casket match at the 1998 Royal Rumble.

was cheered wildly and called "the Show-stopper" and "the Main Event," among other flattering things. On the other hand, Bret Hart, the Canadian national and WWF champion, was labeled a traitor.

Shawn also managed another "first" before Bret. At the October 1997 "Badd Blood" pay-per-view, he faced the Undertaker in the first-ever "Hell in a Cell" match. The winner of this brutal match would face the WWF champ, Bret, in a title bout at the upcoming Survivor Series.

The Hell in a Cell match was the sport's most brutal type of cage match, and by all accounts Shawn had one of the best bouts of his career, proving that no matter what type of match, it was no match for the Heartbreak Kid! When Undertaker's long-lost brother Kane appeared and interfered in the match, Shawn was able to secure the victory and the title match against Bret.

Survivor Series '97 took place in Montreal, Canada, on November 9. Feeling the home court advantage, Bret was out to thwart Shawn's title bid. It looked like that was going to be the case. After a seesaw battle, Bret had Shawn in his famous finishing move, the "sharpshooter." Shawn, however, was able to escape and reverse it. Now, Michaels had turned the tables and had Bret trapped in his own excruciating finisher. Suddenly, the referee called for the bell, saying that Bret had conceded, making the Heartbreak Kid the winner!

The Canadian crowd booed. Controversy reigned as Bret protested, saying he never threw in the towel. But referee Earl Hebner remained adamant that Bret had indeed conceded.

A surprised but grateful Michaels was declared WWF World champion for a third time. For the frustrated Hart it was his last match in the WWF as he soon defected to WCW.

Shawn was riding high again and loving it! He and the other D-Generation X members never had anything nice to say about any of the other wrestlers and often mocked them openly. They thumbed their noses at WWF authority figures like WWF owner Vince McMahon Jr. and WWF commissioner Sergeant Slaughter. Around this time, former Ultimate Fighting champion Ken Shamrock made a bid for Shawn's title. Although he was bigger and more powerful than the Heartbreak Kid, Shamrock failed to strip the gold from Michaels's waist.

"You name the hold, no one can beat me with it," the cocky Michaels bragged to *Wrestling Tourbook*. "I know them all—headlocks, dropkicks, takedowns, flying scissors, reversals, you name it. There is only one Shawn Michaels and I am the greatest athlete who ever crossed the paths of the WWF!"

At the 1998 Royal Rumble Shawn found himself neck deep in his feud with the Undertaker again in, of all things, a casket match. Amazingly, Shawn again proved that specialty matches were his specialty when he beat Undertaker, thanks again to a little help from Kane. Unfortunately for Shawn, however, he injured his back when he was thrown out of the ring and into the coffin. Although he finished the match and emerged victorious, he was in constant pain afterward. "Stone Cold" Steve Austin won the Rumble's Battle Royal, so he was promised a shot at Shawn's title at WrestleMania XIV on March 29, 1998.

Skeptics doubted that Shawn would be able to compete in that match. He had missed some matches leading up to the yearly extravaganza due to his injuries. The wheels had been put in motion, however, and a special referee was hired for the bout—none other than champion boxer Mike Tyson.

Shawn rose to the occasion once again, and had a stellar match with Stone Cold at WrestleMania XIV. The advantage went back and forth and then Shawn went in for the kill. Attempting to deliver some sweet chin music, Shawn launched into the air, but Austin avoided the maneuver and Shawn crashed to the mat on his back, aggravating his injury. Stone Cold took advantage of Shawn's disability and gave him the "Stone Cold stunner," his famous finishing move. With Shawn down on the mat, Tyson made the three-count, giving Austin the victory.

Even though he was in dreadful pain, Shawn gave Tyson an earful and chastised him for not interfering. Tyson returned the favor by hitting Shawn with a right cross to the jaw! Austin rewarded Tyson with a Stone Cold T-shirt. Shawn kissed his third reign goodbye.

Fans did not know it at the time, but this was Shawn's last match in the WWF. Even though he lost, he did not have to hang his head in shame. Most people felt he shouldn't even have been in the match. Besides, getting beaten by champions of the size and ilk of Austin and Tyson was anything but embarrassing. It might be enough to keep another man from returning to the mat sport in any way, but not the Heartbreak Kid!

I t was determined that Shawn would have to be under a doctor's care, and many thought he would need surgery to fix his ailing back. Shawn, however, was hoping to avoid going under the knife, and he embarked on a regimen of rehabilitation under the supervision of the finest doctors in the country. In addition, he furnished his home in San Antonio with orthopedic furniture to help speed his recovery.

On July 13, 1998, the Heartbreak Kid returned to the WWF as a color commentator on *Monday Night Raw*, much to the delight of the crowd and the fans watching at home. The fans were further thrilled when Shawn, an acknowledged master of the microphone, regularly began to join the broadcast team. If he couldn't join the action in the ring, at least he could give his opinions on it.

On August 24, Shawn showed up at *Raw* again. This time he surprised everyone when he got involved in the happenings and saved Chyna from a kiss by big Mark Henry! Afterward, this knight in shining armor added more commentary on the proceedings from the announcers' table.

As good as he was behind the microphone, Shawn knew he was destined for bigger things. This came to pass when he was named WWF commissioner on November 23, 1998, during

---

In 1999, worn down by several career-threatening injuries, Michaels decided to take on a new role outside the ring as commissioner of the WWF.

a *Raw* broadcast. Even though he didn't have an in-ring role, Shawn meant to make his influence felt. His first official act as commissioner was to sanction a match between the Rock and X-Pac. He showed his affiliation with D-Generation X by hanging out with them before the match, but then during the match, Shawn wound up interfering and hitting X-Pac with a chair, thus throwing his lot in with Vince McMahon's Corporation, a newly formed clique of WWF-loyal wrestlers.

Shawn then tried to get other members of D-Generation X to join the Corporation, especially the New Age Outlaws of Jesse James and Billy Gunn. On December 7, it looked as if Shawn had convinced them to join him when, suddenly, they turned their backs on the Corporation and rejoined D-Generation X!

Rubbing salt into Shawn's wounds, the following week D-Generation X, now led by Triple H, parodied the Corporation. Shawn retaliated by scheduling a match between the New Age Outlaws and the Corporation's Big Boss Man and Ken Shamrock. By interfering in the match, Shawn ensured a victory for the Corporation. He also interfered in a match between Triple H and the Rock, but Helmsley's sidekick Chyna was able to keep Shawn from being effective.

Thwarted, Shawn began to use his power as commissioner. In a match where Billy Gunn clearly won the intercontinental title from Corporation member Ken Shamrock, Shawn declared it to be a nontitle match. Of course, Corporation leader Vince McMahon was depending on Shawn to use his power in this way. That's why, the following week, he berated Michaels when he didn't send Corporation

Shawn joined Vince McMahon's Corporation briefly in 1999, but before long he was doing everything possible to thwart the Corporation and help out his wrestler friends.

members to help Shane McMahon, who was being mauled by Mankind. Vince threatened to fire Shawn, and the Heartbreak Kid seemed to be coolly walking away, when he suddenly turned and caught McMahon with some sweet chin music as the crowd went wild.

Not surprisingly, Shawn showed up with D-Generation X the next week and confronted Vince and the rest of the Corporation. Shawn stated that he couldn't be fired, as he had an iron-clad contract. He also used his power as commissioner to make a change to the order of the lineup of the upcoming Royal Rumble, moving Vince from number 30 to number 2, meaning Vince would have to be in the ring with number 1, none other than "Stone Cold" Steve Austin.

Shawn was away from the WWF scene for some time in early 1999 and then it was revealed that he underwent back surgery on January 12, 1999, to fix two disks in his lower back. One week before he was operated on, he told the *San Antonio Express-News*, "It's time to say, 'that's a wrap,'" effectively signaling the end of his active wrestling career.

While he recovered, the Heartbreak Kid continued to throw his weight around, making matches from home that infuriated the Corporation and favored his friends, such as Austin and D-Generation X. For example, on January 25, after Vince McMahon had stepped down as the Rock's number-one contender for the world title, Shawn slyly made Austin the number-one contender, striking another blow against the Corporation!

The Heartbreak Kid continued to make his presence felt, confounding the Corporation at every chance and keeping a high profile. At WrestleMania XV in 1999, for instance, Vince McMahon had named himself the referee for the main-event match between the Rock and Steve Austin, with the intent of getting the Rock the victory. But Shawn used his power as commissioner to reject that idea and wound up leading Vince out of the ring to the sidelines, where he could only watch the action as a spectator.

Michaels's personal life was full of surprises, as well. On March 31, 2000, Shawn, a self-confirmed bachelor, married Rebecca, formerly known as "Whisper" of WCW's Nitro Girls dance team. Then, in partnership with his mentor, Jose Lothario, he opened a wrestling school and a promotion called the Texas Wrestling Alliance (TWA).

Shawn tried to stay active in the WWF, but his outside interests, including the birth of a son, Cameron, kept pulling him away. Still, he ruled on the side of his allies when he could, until giving way to Mick Foley (formerly known as Mankind) who became the new WWF commissioner.

"Shawn Michaels was one of the most gifted athletes I had ever seen," said the voice of the WWF, Jim "J.R." Ross. "This high-strung Texan saw his career end much too soon due to a back injury, but his exploits as a World Wrestling Federation Champion will never be forgotten."

The kudos continue to flow in for the Heartbreak Kid and his absence from the ring leaves a void. And while Michaels seemed to distance himself from the world of professional wrestling, he certainly couldn't be written off. Rumors that he was interested in returning to the WWF circulated.

Michaels continued to make guest appearances for the federation and was widely cheered wherever he appeared. Shawn Michaels was a living WWF legend and its only Grand Slam winner. Experts everywhere agreed that the Heartbreak Kid had been in more five-star matches than any other competitor in the WWF, and that he had earned his place in the record book and wrestling history!

Chronology

1965 Born Michael Shawn Hickenbottom in San Antonio, Texas, on July 22

1984 Makes his pro wrestling debut

1985 Wrestling as "the American Force," Michaels and Paul Diamond win the Texas All-Star Tag Team title

1986 Wins the NWA Central States Tag Team title with Marty Jannetty, as the Midnight Rockers, on May 15

1987 The Midnight Rockers join the AWA and win the AWA World tag team title; they lose the belts to Soldat Ustinov and Boris Zhukov, then win their second AWA World tag team championship from the original Midnight Express on December 27

1988 Enters the WWF with Jannetty as "the Rockers" tag team; the Rockers lose the title to Badd Company on March 19

1992 Wins first WWF Intercontinental championship from British Bulldog on October 27

1993 Loses WWF Intercontinental title to Marty Jannetty; captures second intercontinental title from Jannetty; is stripped of the title for not defending it

1994 With Diesel, defeats the Headshrinkers to win his first WWF World tag team title; the title is declared vacant when Michaels and Diesel split up

1995 Wins third intercontinental title from Jeff Jarrett; wins his first Royal Rumble

1996 Wins first WWF World heavyweight title from Bret Hart, then loses the belt to Psycho Sid

1997 Defeats Sid for his second WWF World heavyweight title; wins second WWF World tag team title with Steve Austin; wins the WWF European title from the British Bulldog; wins third WWF World heavyweight title from Bret Hart

1998 Loses WWF World heavyweight title to Steve Austin; becomes WWF commissioner on November 23

2000 With Jose Lothario, opens a wrestling school and promotion in San Antonio, Texas

Further Reading

Martin, Findlay. "Is That It?" *Power Slam Magazine* (Issue 56, 1999): 24–25.

Hart, Bret. Bret "Hitman" *Hart: The Best There Is, The Best There Was, The Best There Will Ever Be.* North York, Ontario: Stoddart Publishing, 1999.

Hunter, Matt. *Pro Wrestling's Greatest Tag Teams.* Philadelphia: Chelsea House Publishers, 2000.

Hofstede, David. *Slammin': Wrestling's Greatest Heroes and Villains.* Toronto: ECW Press, 1999.

Martin, Twig. "Shawn Michaels vs. Bret Hart." *Wrestling World Magazine* (December 1996): 49–55.

Index

Photo Credits

The Acci'Dent: pp. 2, 6, 10, 13, 20, 30, 35, 38, 44, 47, 50, 54, 57, 60; Jeff Eisenberg Sports Photography: pp. 16, 19, 22, 24, 32, 42.

STEPHEN CIACCIARELLI is the former editor of *Wrestling World* magazine and the author of numerous books on pro wrestling, including Ringside Wrestling's *The Champions* and *Great Grudge Matches*. He is currently the Ringside Chat columnist for the Huddlin' With The Pros sports website (*www.huddlin.com*) and a freelance writer for various wrestling magazines. He lives in New York City.